First published in 2008 by
New Holland Publishers (UK) Ltd
London • Cape Town • Sydney • Auckland

www.newhollandpublishers.com

Garfield House
86–88 Edgware Road
London
W2 2EA
United Kingdom

80 McKenzie Street
Cape Town 8001
South Africa

Unit 1, 66 Gibbes Street
Chatswood, NSW 2067
Australia

218 Lake Road
Northcote
Auckland
New Zealand

ISBN: 978 1 84773 077 0

Photography, graphic design and editorial direction: Marcos Zimmermann
Prologue and text: Tomás Eloy Martínez
Translation of poetry: Amanda Hopkinson
Design operator: Juan Carlos López
Assistant photographer: Mariano Zimmermann
Photographs developed by: Professional Color
Proof reading: Gabriela Ventureira
Color separations: Dot Prepress
Printed in Spain

PATAGONIA

Nature's Last Frontier

Photographs and editorial direction

Marcos Zimmermann

Prologue and text

Tomás Eloy Martínez

NEW
HOLLAND

Route 6. Near Esperanza, Province of Santa Cruz.

There is something that the photographs of Marcos Zimmermann catch on the wing, and yet defy description with the elusiveness of mercury: a metaphysical beauty that lies not in the landscape but in the excess of landscape, at an extreme beyond the reach of language. There are times when words are defeated by the categorical force of reality, falling nowhere, overcome by the weight of their own emptiness.

For centuries, explorers have tried to explain Patagonia. What was this endless steppe, with grasses flattened by the seething wind, beyond which rose peaks and lakes where lay – so they believed – an earthly garden of Eden?

"Infinite plains create illusions, mirages", wrote Charles Darwin, when in 1834 he ventured across the barren plains of Santa Cruz. "The similarity of the scenery acts as an irritant to me. Everywhere we see the same birds and insects. The curse of sterility is on the land."

In the depths of this indifferent land, Antonio Pigafetta had, however, spied giants as he sailed by with Magellan's expedition, "formidable towers of flesh" guarding a blinding fortress of burnished silver: the City of the Caesars.

In the beginning, giants appeared in all reports, ever since the *Mundus Novus* (1503), attributed to Amerigo Vespucci, which apparently gave rise to the legend of the prodigious Patagonians. Vespucci, or whoever usurped his name, had never travelled south of the Gulf of San Julián, but nevertheless told in *Mundus Novus* that one afternoon, close to the untamed seas of the South Pole, his ships sighted a small group of female giants, "well proportioned, three young and two old", who became ashamed of their nakedness when they found themselves observed by their minuscule intruders. Sailors wove a net, and devised ruses to be able to catch them. As they stalked their prey, thirty-six robust, well-built men "so well-proportioned and agreeable they were pleasing to the eye", scared them away with sticks and arrows, chasing them into the sea with their enormous feet as light as clouds.

Solitude guarded by such immoderately large beings should by rights be in itself disproportionate. In the two centuries following the discovery, unexplored Patagonia became the site of every utopia: there lay Paradise, the Source of Eternal Youth, the Golden Calf and the Crown of Thorns. Not until the rationalism of the 18th century did the vast steppe recover its original pristine beauty, its emptiness and unpeopled perfection. And for it, in turn, to become a place outside time, with an unknown past and a future from which nothing was expected.

Louis-Antoine de Bougainville, in his voyage around the world, did not even dare approach the Patagonian shore. In his memoirs, published in 1771 – mandatory reading for encyclopedists – he mentioned the raging storms that destroyed his vessel's foremast and threatened to bring down the mainmast, made careful note of the longitude and latitude he had reached, and then turned around, fearful of the silence and the devilish wings he could hear beating in the darkness. Defeated by the terrors of his imagination, he sailed to the Falkland Islands (Malvinas), which he also found desolate, but lacking in mystery.

Bougainville is the first in a long line of explorers who catalogued with Positivist zeal everything they came across. Where he saw only tides, undertows and reefs, the rest recorded guanacos, foxes, porphyry pebbles, condors, cormorants, penguins and geese. Darwin was disturbed by ill-humour and the unexpected changes in the natural order. George Chaworth Musters, who in 1871 chronicled the details of his life among the Tehuelches, was surprised by the favourable disposition with which they faced the hostile desert, by the devotion of their conjugal love and the coquettish nature of their women. Francisco P. Moreno, the *Perito* (expert), gathered together all this knowledge into a kind of treatise, a journal of an illness and a report to the authorities that included a description of the theology and languages of Patagonia, and an inventory of its flora, glaciers, lakes, winds and cooking habits. "The mysterious plain has shed its veil," wrote Moreno. "Where others found disillusion, we are now able to admire shining beauty."

Moreno was the first to note the conjunction of two conflicting geographies: the fertile west, with its string of rainbow-hued lakes, transformed into jewels – emeralds, rubies, opals – by the mineral residues of eternity, and its trail of mountains, jagged as lightning, capitals of ice and forests of stone thrown up by seas a hundred thousand years ago. On the other side, to the east, lies the outline of a barren coast, sown with shells and rocks, dunes and hawthorn, and beyond, crazed clutches of festuca grasses, flying nowhere in the wind, penguin and seal colonies, petrels and pregnant whales seeking sheltered bays in which to hold their thunderous calving.

Between the eastern and western extremes, the horizon is ill-defined: plains pounded by the sudden droves of wild horses in their frantic search for rich grassland, condors descending from the freezing skies to seize a baby guanaco, unexpected streams, water meadows, rivers of sulphate, imaginary forests created by distant mirages, implacable hills, oil rigs and tongues of dust coming and going in the wind without rhyme or reason.

In the past, travellers complained of the monotony of these places. They could travel league after league without anything changing, or sometimes, suddenly – on crossing the central plain, for example – everything began to seem other than what it was. However, it is not monotony, but simple immensity. In endless space, everything looks the same because geography stretches out too slowly, the earth smoothes its folds as if it had just awoken, and when by chance a hill is spied, it seems to have dropped there through an oversight of God.

Like the sea, like deserts of sand, the barren horizon of Patagonia is but another form of labyrinth. When it lost its role as a medieval utopia, as an impossible dream, its desolate regions became a refuge for crazed and desperate souls.

In mid-1858, Orllie-Antoine de Tounens, a French lawyer whose imagination had been fired by travellers' tales, ventured among the Tehuelche Indians in the southern Andes, declaring himself the monarch of that endless kingdom. Two years later, as he rested under the shade of an appletree, a Chilean patrol captured him and brought him back to reality.

Almost at the same time, two hundred Welsh colonists discovered in Patagonia the unexpected paradise that others had found so elusive. They were fleeing from poverty and the unyielding censorship that the British Crown had imposed on the spread of their language. In the valley of the Chubut River, where the air is always fresh and clear, they built their modest brick dwellings and wove a firm friendship with the Indians in the region, whose meekness belied all tales of savagery. Along the banks of the Chubut River they founded a line of towns with reminiscences of Wales: Madryn, Trelew, Gaiman, Dolavon, where time stands still, even today, at tea-time.

In 1901, the parents of Juan Domingo Perón, unsure of where they were headed, came ashore close to the bay of whales, and set out over the dunes on a cart. Fearing the ravages of thirst, they carried with them two large barrels of water. During their trek, they felt that the horizon was an enormous sheet of rust and stone. They began to imagine that the solitude would devour them with the viciousness of a prehistoric animal. Three years later, disenchanted with the coast, they headed into a fertile, desolate valley in Santa Cruz, in the far south, in a hollow surrounded by clusters of pine and araucaria trees. Where there was nothing, hope filled every uninhabited corner.

Dreams of an unattainable freedom summoned the famed trio of bandits formed by Etta Place, Butch Cassidy and the Sundance Kid to these same latitudes at around the same time. They had adopted the life of respectable cattle farmers in Chubut, but according to Etta, eventually the unbroken sameness of the days undermined their spirits. In January 1905 they appeared suddenly in Río Gallegos, where they held up the Bank of London. They then fled north, which was their undoing. After they crossed the Colorado River, marking the imaginary boundary of Patagonia, they became caught up in madness. A detachment of Bolivian troops ended their lives in a small town in Potosí, close to the Los Frailes range.

Patagonia is so empty, so vast, that no-one has been able to see it all. It occupies almost 800,000 square kilometres (312,000 square miles), a size that is hard to imagine. Trucks sometimes roll for days at a time without coming across a soul. Across the eastern half, lacking the shelter of valleys and woodland, the wind blows freely and furiously, unceasing, maddening. In the west, the dust settles and the beauty is from another world. Lakes succeed each other from San Martín de los Andes to the glaciers close to Calafate, which create an improbable forest of ice, breaking apart every four years with a volcanic roar.

Then there are the Andes. They stand, broken by mountain passes and gorges, blocking the way of the clouds, forcing them to feed the mountain slopes. Myrtles, raspberries, strawberries, wheat, vineyards and olive groves: at the slightest sign of life, nature lays aside the hostility to which it has grown accustomed on the coast and spills out over vales and valleys.

In the last half-century, these lands have once again become utopia. Following the migratory flows that depopulated the countryside during the Second World War, cities became a source of growing disenchantment. Thousands of young people began to look south, where happiness still seemed possible. The coastal areas saw the arrival of people seeking to put down roots, hold a steady job, bring up a family. The adventurous, those who felt the pull of the land, headed west. There were already settlements of Swiss, Austrians and Germans around the lakes. Further away there was uninhabited, fertile land that acted as a magnet for the hippie community. Hundreds built log cabins on the shores of the Azul River. Others sought refuge in El Bolsón, where they became gold and silversmiths. Survivors of this era can still be seen in the local markets, their physique weathered by the thirst for freedom that they had gone to find, and perhaps did.

Memories are everywhere in Patagonia. People go there to collect them, under the snow or in the summer brilliance, and they take them away, caught in their hair, or in their pockets. Memories are fleeting, however. The wind blows and uproots them. There are memories on every shore, but just as they appear, so do they vanish. They become fake eggs to be hatched by male penguins, clumps of grass tangled in a dust storm, photograph albums of honeymoons, school graduation trips, first loves. This vastness where everything happens is also a vastness where everything passes, flies, departs. Memories cannot remain where time does not exist, and in Patagonia, time has vanished. The past dissolves into the present, the present becomes the future. Hence the achievement of these photographs, which capture the wind in flight, seize time, immobilize it, surprising eternity at the exact moment when it turns and shows its face.

Tomás Eloy Martínez

Every single step forward felt like a huge achievement. Gale force winds were being channelled through the sheer valley walls of the Fitzroy range, and with each large gust, it was as if we were being blown three steps back from our destination; the summit of the glacial moraine ridge. Our quest to view the azure- coloured glacial lake was going to be somewhat of a struggle. However this was to be expected in Patagonia, a place where nothing is easy. A land where struggle is an essential part of everyday life.

Spanning the southern tip of the South American continent, Patagonia is a landscape of extremes divided by the backbone of the magnificent Andean mountain range. Tierra del Fuego in the deep south is host to Cape Horn, the southernmost point of the continent and not, in fact, a true cape but actually part of the island archipelago that forms the region of Tierra del Fuego. Heading north from the icy expanse of Antarctica, this group of islands is the first glimpse of the Andes as they rise dramatically from the Southern Ocean to form this great continent.

Tierra del Fuego gained its colourful name from the first European explorer to visit the archipelago. Ferdinand Magallen named the land the 'Island of Fires' in 1520 as a result of the numerous fires visible on the main island, which he believed were an attempt by the Native American Indians to lure his crew to the land and ambush them as they entered the dense forests. Little did he realize that the Yamana Indians actually relied upon the primeval fire to provide them with warmth in these sub-antarctic lands, and that they would even carry a lighted fire aboard their canoes when they were hunting and fishing, as they often wore very little or no clothing.

Vast glaciers and dense, highland forests still cover this jagged, mountainous landscape and offer numerous opportunities for the modern-day explorer to get off the beaten track. Some of the more accessible hikes begin near Ushuaia, the self pro-claimed southernmost city in the world and the international gateway for Antarctica expeditions. My own experiences of hiking in the great Lenga forests of the nearby Tierra Del Fuego National Park were to empower me with a huge respect for the Patagonian flora and fauna.

After a hard day of exploring the varied landscape of the park on foot, we had pitched our tent at a location in the national park alongside the Beagle channel. As the daylight quickly faded and the transition to dusk began, I noticed a pair of eyes staring at us in our campsite from deep within the woodland. As the creature began to approach, I caught my first sighting of a Patagonian grey fox, wearing a fur coat so dense that it could have easily been mistaken for a wolf. This majestic wild animal took a few minutes to confirm if we were a threat (or a potential food source) before finally walking away into the darkness. We were privileged to have been accepted into the creature's domain – although we were probably never trusted.

The ownership of Tierra del Fuego is divided between two countries, Argentina and Chile. This pattern is repeated along the length of the Patagonian region, with the imposing peaks of the Andes forming a natural boundary between the two.

The climate of the region changes dramatically – a clear transition can be experienced from the wetter, windblown western landscape to the drier eastern areas which sit within the rain shadow of the world's longest terrestrial mountain range. Straddling and partially engulfing the lofty peaks of the Andes, the southern Patagonia icefield is the largest region of glaciers to be found within the southern hemisphere outside of Antarctica, and provides a sheer contrast to the lush green environment of southern Chile and the sun-drenched barren landscape of southern Argentina. Covering an amazing 13,000 square kilometers (5,020 square miles) the southern Patagonia icefield actually once covered an area nearly forty times bigger. The legacy of this retreating sheet of ice has been the scouring of the landscape, and the formation of the majestic fjords to be found along the coast of Chile. As the ice cap continues to retreat, it in turn reveals a landscape which has been covered by ice for over 10,000 years.

However, it is not just glaciation and the existence of icefields that have made their mark on the landscapes of southern Patagonia. Plate tectonics and the subduction of the Nazca plate underneath the South American plate has resulted in an uplift that has created what has to be considered some of the most dramatic mountain scenery to be found anywhere in the world. Without a doubt, one of the best ways to experience these landforms is on foot. It was whilst I was hiking the 'Circuit' track of the Torres del Paine National Park in Chile that I viewed some of these astounding landscapes in close proximity. After a particularly arduous climb over a mountain pass encountered mid-way through the eight day hike circling the national park, battling yet again with the infamous Patagonian wind, I finally managed to reach the summit of the pass and was immediately rewarded with a birds' eye view of the southern Patagonia ice field – an unforgettable vision of an immense sea of ice blanketing the landscape, continuing as far as the eye could see.

The hike continued for nearly two days alongside a relatively small stretch of the icefield, offering a vantage point that was essential to comprehend the full extent of its size. Briefly after the route began to leave the glacier and started to head inland, I was yet again to see a landscape that left me in awe. The convoluted, granite horns of the Cuernos del Paine dominated the gently, undulating land-mass that surrounded the mountain range. Far in the distance I could just make out the towering pillars of the Torres piercing the clouds that seem to eternally shroud the peaks.

In Argentina, the pillars of the Fitzroy range are strikingly similar to the Torres del Paine. Located within the northern boundary of the Los Glaciers National Park, it is not surprising that the range offers good hiking opportunities. However, here the weather is particularly fickle, even by Patagonia standards – which in the past led to Mount Fitzroy (also known as Cerro Chaltén) being considered one of the most difficult mountains to climb in the world. The reality is that unless you are very lucky you will be welcomed to Cerro Chaltén by rain and winds. If you are fortunate, the weather may clear just long enough for you to see the infamous peak.

Life and death are never very far apart for the inhabitants of Patagonia. As Guanacos graze on the hardy grasses and shrubs clinging for survival on the wind-scoured Patagonian steppes, they maintain the vigil of keeping their senses aware to the possible presence of predators, especially the puma. High in the sky, the enigmatic Andean condor can often be seen waiting for its next meal to win its fight for life in this unrelenting landscape. This vulture, alongside the other carrion eaters to be found in Patagonia, feeds entirely upon the dead of the land. There is no need for this majestic bird, whose wingspan measures over 2.5 metres (8.2 feet), to hunt – all that is required is patience.

The Andes continue to craft and manipulate the landscape to the highest elevations a condor can fly. East of the range, traveling north by road through the Patagonian steppe is a challenging and dusty affair along frequently unsealed and corrugated roads. Traversing hundreds of kilometers through this barren environment is a slow process, but perhaps one of the only true ways to appreciate this land of vast, far horizons with little signs of human habitation apart from the occasional homestead. At the same latitude but located to the west in Chile, the temperate rainforest engulfs the foothills of the Andes and the almost perpetual rain continues to flood and wash away the basic road infrastructure. This is a landscape thriving with life, in complete contrast to the dry Patagonia of the west.

A few hundred kilometers further north, an almost surreal transformation occurs. The barren steppe gives way to pockets of ancient woodland scattered between azure-coloured lakes. Dry, dusty soil is transformed into a fertile land perfect for farming and human habitation. Perfectly symmetrical active volcanoes also begin to dominate the horizon, a reminder of their ability to reclaim the land. Amongst numerous large lakes and surrounded by dense forests with new and ancient growth, you are submerged in an environment so alive that you soon begin to forget the Patagonia of the south. These wild lands are far more conducive to the nurture of life.

The Lake District region of northern Patagonia combines these areas of Argentina and Chile to create a lush, fertile environment of semi-wilderness that offers the visitor a number of delights. With an influx of tourists, a new improved infrastructure of travel has been unveiled to allow easy exploration. Navigation between Argentina and Chile is possible by regular boat sailings within the lakes. The brave explorer may even hike in the ancient woodlands between the two official entry points of the countries, proof that this landscape is so vast that even man has not felt the urge to tame it.

I have fond memories of bush camping within the Nahuel Huapi National Park in Argentina. Far from the madding crowd, the bright constellations of the southern night sky provided hours of natural entertainment. We were also lucky to witness the appearance of the comet McNaught, believed to be the brightest comet in over 40 years. It could be seen with the naked eye and dominated the vast and open skies for several nights, with only the occasional call of an owl diverting our attention. Here, so far from civilization, our thoughts expanded to the possible viewing of a puma hunting in its natural environment and, although we never experienced this, we did enjoy a somewhat safer encounter with an armadillo hiding in the dense scrub.

Travel in Patagonia dictates that you are flexible with your plans and that you allow for the unexpected. Perhaps the most overwhelming sensation for the traveller is of visiting a land at the mercy of the forces of nature. The harsh extremes of the fickle weather ensure that human habitation is limited to certain regions and that passage over this wild land is confined to minimal routes. Snow and gale-force winds are common even during the summer months, rendering preparation and foresight essential for even the briefest of trips into the great wild open.

Despite the harshness of this region, Patagonia is undeniably a gem of the world. Yes, determination is required from the visitor to gain the most from the region, and life is by no means easy for its inhabitants. But, when you do finally take the last step to the tip of the ridge and see the crystal clear waters of the azure lake, you realize that the struggle to reach the top was worth it to appreciate the wild grandeur of the place. Whilst struggle may be a part of everyday life in Patagonia, it is by no means a negative sensation. Indeed, it may be the very reason that Patagonia endures in the fond memories of the visitor.

Jason Friend

Inside a carriage of the 'Trochita' train. Esquel, Province of Chubut.

Route 40. Pampa del Asador, Province of Santa Cruz.

Agujas de sol, viajes desorientados de la intemperie, vientos, otoños vacíos.
Aquí está el centro del mundo, pero no hay mundo. Es sólo un espacio preñado
del mundo que alguna vez será. ¿Lo ves? Estas claridades cegadoras
lo están anunciando.

Pinpricks of sunlight; empty winds of autumn; wayward journeys of unsettled weather.
The apex of the world is here, the world itself vanishes. Only space remains, pregnant
with a world as yet unborn. Do you see it? These blinding interludes herald the event.

1

Previous page: Bluff. Between Pico Truncado and Las Heras, Province of Santa Cruz.

Open country. Between Puerto Deseado and Jaramillo, Province of Santa Cruz.

El Pedral Beach. Province of Chubut.

Near Tar Lake. Province of Santa Cruz.

Hill-top. Province of Santa Cruz.

Previous page: Bluff near Lake Cardiel. Province of Santa Cruz.

Nunca se sabrá qué manos han dibujado estos vellones: si las del aire que se
ha marchado o las del relámpago que los baña cada vez que pasa por allí,
el relámpago que no los deja alzar la cabeza y mirar hacia Dios. Ahora se sabe
de dónde les viene tanta melancolía.

The hands that sketched these woolly fleeces will forever remain anonymous: perhaps
they belong to the passing breeze, perhaps to the lightning flashes immersing them in
sudden light, blinding those who would raise their heads and see God. At last we have
learnt from where they draw their intense melancholy.

2

Previous page: Plain with grasses. Between Jaramillo and Gobernador Moyano, Province of Santa Cruz.

Desertification. Province of Santa Cruz.

Meseta Cascajosa. Province of Santa Cruz.

Grassy hill. Province of Santa Cruz.

Cliffs. Between Gualjaina and Paso del Sapo, Province of Chubut.

Previous page: Plateau near Puerto Deseado. Province of Santa Cruz.

Las piedras tienen, a veces, la condición de la música. Son un reino inmóvil que fluye hacia el pasado, una pereza que no descansa. Todos los días, las piedras cumplen otros cien años.

At times even the stones assume the quality of music. A motionless realm flowing into the past, a lassitude that never ceases. Day on day the stones celebrate another century.

3

Previous page: Piedra Clavada. Province of Santa Cruz.

Fossilized tree in the Petrified Forests Natural Monument. Province of Santa Cruz.

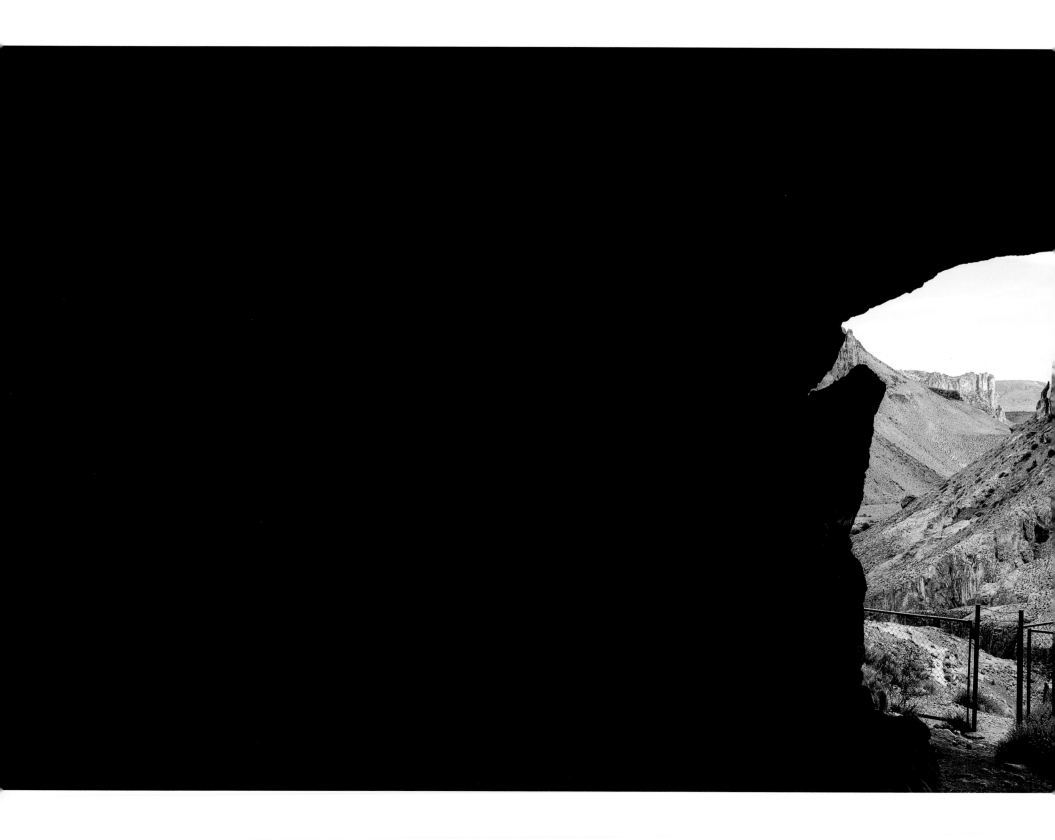

Gorge on the Pinturas River seen from the Cueva de las Manos. Province of Santa Cruz.

Painted hands in the Cueva de las Manos. Province of Santa Cruz.

47

Shore of the San Matías Gulf. Province of Chubut.

Previous page: Hills. Near Valle Encantado, Province of Neuquén.

¿De qué otro desamparo huye el agua que se refugia en este desamparo? Huye de lo visible hacia lo invisible, de las ciudades llenas de tiempo hacia el aire sin tiempo, huye de la historia y de la memoria para rehacerse a sí misma, el agua, en esta realidad de la que ha desaparecido la realidad.

From whatever barren waste flees the water seeking refuge in this barren waste? It flows from the visible towards the invisible, from cities filled with time to the air that knows no history. The water flees memory to rebirth into a new reality from which our present version has evaporated.

4

Previous page: Beach at Monte León. Province of Santa Cruz.

Puerto Deseado Estuary. Province of Santa Cruz.

Cabo Blanco. Province of Santa Cruz.

Beach on the San Matías Gulf. Province of Chubut.

Previous page: Cliffs near El Doradillo. Valdés Peninsula, Province of Chubut.

Cabo Dos Bahías. Camarones, Province of Chubut.

Caleta Valdés. Valdés Peninsula, Province of Chubut.

Rock formations opposite Puerto Deseado. Province of Santa Cruz.

Cliffs. Province of Santa Cruz.

Monte León Island. Province of Santa Cruz.

Walking on the Perito Moreno Glacier. Province of Santa Cruz.

Previous page: Tributary of the Deseado River. Province of Santa Cruz.

Tanta blancura oculta todo el color, todas las formas. La transparencia, la quietud, la herida de la luz permite ver mejor. Las estrellas se abrieron y lo que cayó está aquí: en estos lagos, en estos hielos, en estas sombras blancas.

So much whiteness obliterates all shape, all colour. There is transparency, tranquillity, a wounding light to enhance our vision. The stars parted, and all that fell landed here, in these lakes, these icy wastes, these white shadows.

5

Previous page: Perito Moreno Glacier. Los Glaciares National Park, Province of Santa Cruz.

Lower part of the Perito Moreno Glacier. Province of Santa Cruz.

Mount Fitz Roy. Province of Santa Cruz.

Previous page: Lake Guillelmo. Province of Río Negro.

Limay River. Province of Río Negro.

Beagle Channel and Ushuaia. Province of Tierra del Fuego.

Beaver colonies and trees. Province of Tierra del Fuego.

Previous page: Surroundings of Cerro Catedral. Province of Río Negro.

Todo fue mar alguna vez, todo es ahora nostalgia del mar distante. Lo que aquí
debajo yace es sólo el cielo con sus costas, la niñez del cielo, los canales que
fueron nubes alguna vez y que ahora duermen sobre sus lechos de luz,
a la vuelta de tantos viajes.

*Once upon a time all was ocean, today all is but yearning for a distant sea. What lies
here below is no more than a sky rimmed by shorelines, heaven in its infancy. Those
runnels descended from the clouds now recline on beds of light, homeward returned from
many journeys.*

6

Previous page: Lake District. Province of Río Negro.

Laguna del Desierto. Province of Santa Cruz.

Lake Argentino. Province of Santa Cruz.

Lapataia Bay. Province of Tierra del Fuego.

Lake Nahuel Huapi. Province of Río Negro.

Branch of the Las Vueltas River. Province of Santa Cruz.

Elephant seal at Punta Delgada. Valdés Peninsula, Province of Chubut.

Previous page: Deseado River at dusk. Province of Santa Cruz.

Seres que han ido y han vuelto de Dios. Aves de muchos nombres, elefantes, lobos, criaturas de naturaleza indecisa, ¿cómo hacen para que, aun cuando aletean y chillan y braman, el aire sea de vidrio: puro silencio?

Beings which have departed and returned to God. Innumerable unnamed birds, walruses, sea-elephants and sea-wolves, creatures of indeterminate nature. In the face of this beating of wings, of squawks and roars, how come the air withstands in crystal silence?

7

Previous page: Right whale opposite Puerto Pirámide. Valdés Peninsula, Province of Chubut.

Elephant seals. Valdés Peninsula, Province of Chubut.

Penguin colonies. Cabo Dos Bahías Nature Reserve, Province of Chubut.

Cormorant nesting ground. Punta León, Province of Chubut.

Milodón River. Near El Chaltén, Province of Santa Cruz.

Previous page: Seagulls. Province of Chubut.

Quién podría apartar los ojos de tanta efervescencia, tanta pasión y oro que van brotándole al mundo, como suspiros.

Who can look away from such effervescence, such passion, from the gold that bursts forth and showers the worlds with sighs?

8

Previous page: Shores of Lake Buenos Aires. Province of Santa Cruz.

Road between farms. Province of Santa Cruz.

Low land. Between Tolhuin and Ushuaia, Province of Tierra del Fuego.

125

Lengas in autumn. Province of Tierra del Fuego.

Previous page: Farm. Los Antiguos, Province of Santa Cruz.

Grasslands. Between El Chaltén and Laguna del Desierto, Province of Santa Cruz.

132

Lake Puelo. Province of Chubut.

Abandoned train station. Near Las Heras, Province of Santa Cruz.

Previous page: El Chaltén and Mount Fitz Roy. Province of Santa Cruz.

Son ínfimas señales, apenas guiños del paso de la especie: barcos, aldeas, despojos, a veces cabañas solitarias, la voz del que ha estado acá y, yéndose, se ha quedado. Los seres humanos son, bajo esta luz, otra ilusión de la naturaleza.

Minute signs of a species passing in the blink of an eye: boats, villages, an occasional isolated cabin, traces of people who once were here, the voice of a man which remained after him. In this fierce light humanity is exposed as another natural illusion.

9

Previous page: Street in El Chaltén. Province of Santa Cruz.

Chenque Hill and Comodoro Rivadavia. Province of Chubut.

Puerto Deseado. Province of Santa Cruz.

Wind farm. Near Comodoro Rivadavia, Province of Chubut.

Oil well. Province of Neuquén.

Car cemetery. Province of Chubut.

Burning rubbish in the outskirts of Comodoro Rivadavia. Province of Chubut.

En la otra página de la nada está Adán. La vida está empezando aquí, en el punto donde todo parecía haber terminado.

On the page facing the void Adam appears. Life starts here, just where we thought it was all over.

Gauchos herding a flock of sheep. Province of Chubut.

Page 152/153: Buildings in Comodoro Rivadavia. Province of Chubut.

Contents